The Best ✅ W9-AZQ-425
of
Cajun - Creole Recipes

by
Theresa Nell Millang

Published by
Adventure Publications, Incorporated
P.O. Box 269
Cambridge, MN 55008

1-800-678-7006

FOREWORD

Cajun-Creole cookery can best be described as an inclusion of all food—prepared in a special way. As you page through this comprehensive Cajun-Creole cookbook, you will find that most recipes are not hot and spicy—as is often perceived. You will discover that Cajuns and Creoles eat tons of rice! A typical kitchen will always have fresh onions, garlic, bell pepper, celery, parsley and green onions on hand. The spices will include black, white and red ground pepper. File' (pronounced fee-lay) is an herb made from sassafras leaves. The herb is used in some gumbos—usually plain chicken gumbo. Thyme is another herb frequently used. Hot pepper sauce is usually found on the table—not in the prepared food. This allows you to set your own limit!

The Cajuns (short for Acadians), a French speaking people, left Nova Scotia some 200 years ago—refusing to swear allegiance to the king of England; many settled in Louisiana. Creoles came to Louisiana directly from France, long before the Cajuns. Creole dishes have more of a true French influence, at least there was a time when that was true. Today however, it is hard to distinguish between Cajun and Creole dishes, both are so inter-mixed—like the people themselves.

I grew up in Louisiana. My mother was a wonderful cook. Cajun-Creole cooking was always served at our house. I watched mother prepare the delicious meals, and I later drew from her expertise. I hope you will enjoy this collection of recipes. Bon appetit'!

TABLE OF CONTENTS

SEAFOOD

VEGETABLES AND DRESSINGS

DESSERTS AND SWEETS

MISCELLANEOUS

BOUDIN BLANC

4 cups salted water
1½ pounds lean pork
½ pound pork liver
4 cups cooked white rice
2 cups finely chopped onions
½ cup chopped bell pepper
½ cup chopped parsley
½ cup chopped green onion tops
1 teaspoon ground red pepper
½ teaspoon black pepper
1¼ teaspoons salt
Sausage casings

Put water in a large pot. Add lean pork; bring to a boil. Reduce heat, cover, and cook for 1 hour. Add pork liver; cook 20 minutes. Remove from pot. Cool, then coarsely grind together. Place in a large bowl. Add rice, chopped vegetables, and seasonings. Mix well. Use a sausage stuffer to fill casings. Do not over-stuff. Tie ends of casing. Place into slow-boiling water. Cook 2 minutes. Reduce heat; simmer for 3 minutes. Cut into serving pieces 2 to 3 inches long. Serve warm or cold. Keep refrigerated. Serves 6 to 8.

CRAB DIP

3 tablespoons butter
4 tablespoons minced onion
1 cup fresh mushrooms, sliced
   cooked, and drained
$\frac{1}{4}$ cup all-purpose flour
$1\frac{1}{4}$ cups milk

Dash of Tabasco sauce
$\frac{1}{2}$ teaspoon salt
Black pepper to taste
$\frac{1}{2}$ teaspoon prepared mustard
1 cup Cheddar cheese, grated
1 pound fresh crab meat

Heat butter in saucepan. Add onion; stir and cook until wilted. Add mushrooms; stir and cook 2 minutes. Add flour; blend well. Stir in milk, Tabasco, salt, pepper, and mustard. Add cheese; blend until melted. Add crab meat; simmer until cooked. Serves 10.

CRAB MEAT PARTY OMELETTE

12 slices bacon
3 tablespoons corn oil
1 cup diced bell pepper
½ cup chopped onion
6 eggs, beaten
1 cup cream

⅛ teaspoon black pepper
Few grains ground red pepper
¼ pound Swiss cheese, diced
1 6-oz. can crab meat
1 teaspoon salt

Fry bacon until crisp; drain. Crumble and set aside. Heat oil in medium skillet; stir and cook bell pepper and onion until tender. Set aside. Grease the inside of a 9-inch springform pan with additional oil; place on a baking sheet. Combine eggs, cream, seasonings, cheese, crab meat, salt, bacon, bell pepper, and onions. Pour into preheated pan. Bake uncovered in preheated 450-degree oven for 10 minutes. Reduce heat to 350 degrees. Bake 12 minutes. Remove sides from pan. Cut into 16 wedges.

CRAB-STUFFED MUSHROOMS

2 dozen large fresh mushrooms
4 tablespoons butter
2 cloves garlic, minced
3 tablespoons minced onion
½ pound cooked crab meat
2 eggs, beaten
2 tablespoons mayonnaise

3 tablespoons seasoned dried
  bread crumbs
3 tablespoons minced green
  onion tops
1 teaspoon fresh lemon juice
Salt and pepper to taste
Parmesan cheese

Remove stems from cleaned mushrooms; chop stems and saute in butter with garlic and onion. Brush mushrooms with melted butter. Mix together crab meat, eggs, mayonnaise, bread crumbs, green onion tops, lemon juice, salt and pepper, add to onion and garlic mixture and cook 5 minutes. Fill mushrooms with mixture. Sprinkle with cheese. Bake in buttered shallow glass casserole for 15 minutes in a 400-degree oven. Serve warm. Makes 2 dozen.

CRAWFISH BOIL

15 pounds live crawfish
1 teaspoon crushed red pepper
4 bay leaves, crumbled
1 tablespoon allspice

3 tablespoons mustard seed
1 teaspoon whole cloves
2 tablespoons whole coriander
1/4 teaspoon black pepper

Put crawfish in a tub; wash with clean water. In an extra-large pot, bring 5 quarts of water to a full rolling boil. Make a bag out of cheesecloth; put all the seasonings in bag; tie. Place bag in the boiling water. Drop a few pounds of crawfish at a time in full boiling water. Cover pot. Return water to a bull boil. Cook about 5 minutes. Remove from water. Serve on a large platter. Let everyone peel their own. If you like a milder flavor, omit bag of seasonings. Boil as above. Serve with white vinegar, salt, and black pepper. Serve the seasoned crawfish with cocktail sauce. Serves 6.

MARINATED CRABS

2 dozen fresh crabs, boiled
  and cleaned
1½ cups Italian dressing
¾ cup olive oil
⅓ cup wine vinegar
½ cup chopped celery
1 cup green onions, chopped

6 cloves garlic, chopped
½ cup sliced dill pickles
½ cup stuffed green olives
1 teaspoon Tabasco sauce
1 cup fresh shrimp, cooked
  and cleaned
Salt to taste

Cut crabs in half; remove claws. Combine all ingredients except crab and shrimp, mixing marinade well. Place crabs, claws and shrimp in a large bowl. Pour marinade over all. Refrigerate for at least 12 hours. Serves 6.

OVEN-BARBECUED SHRIMP

8 tablespoons butter
1/3 cup Worcestershire sauce
1 teaspoon thyme
1 teaspoon rosemary
1 teaspoon black pepper
1 teaspoon Tabasco sauce

2 lemons, sliced
1 teaspoon salt
2 cloves garlic, minced
1 teaspoon olive oil
4 pounds large shrimp with heads on; unpeeled

Melt butter in saucepan. Add all ingredients except shrimp. Mix well. Put shrimp in shallow pan. Pour marinade over shrimp. Marinate in refrigerator for 2 hours. Bake uncovered in marinade at 400 degrees for 25 minutes. Serves 6.

SHRIMP REMOULADE

4 tablespoons horseradish
  mustard
½ cup tarragon vinegar
3 tablespoons catsup
1 tablespoon paprika
1 teaspoon salt
½ teaspoon ground red pepper
2 tablespoons chopped parsley

1 clove garlic, chopped
½ cup olive oil
½ cup chopped green onions
½ cup chopped celery
2 pounds boiled shrimp,
  peeled and deveined
Lettuce

Combine all ingredients except shrimp in a blender or mixer bowl; blend throughly. Pour mixture over shrimp placed in a glass bowl. Marinate 4 to 12 hours in refrigerator, stirring a few times. Serve over a bed of shredded lettuce. Serve with crackers and seasoned bread sticks. Serves 6.

SHRIMP TOAST

12 slices thin bread
1 pound raw shrimp, peeled
  and coarsely chopped
½ cup finely diced onion
1 tablespoon minced bell pepper
2 teaspoons salt
¼ teaspoon red pepper sauce

1 teaspoon sugar
1 tablespoon cornstarch
1 egg, beaten
1 5-oz. can water chestnuts,
  finely chopped
Flavored dry bread crumbs
Corn oil for frying

Trim crust off bread; discard. Mix together all ingredients, except 12 slices of bread, corn oil, and bread crumbs. Spread mixture on bread; sprinkle with dry bread crumbs. Cut bread into triangles or squares. Heat enough corn oil to deep-fry. If using an electric skillet, fill with 1½ inches corn oil, and heat to 350-375 degrees. Fry shrimp-side down first; turn over and fry until golden brown. Drain on paper towel. Makes about 4 dozen.

CHICKEN-OYSTER-SAUSAGE GUMBO

8 tablespoons corn oil
8 tablespoons flour
1 large onion, chopped
8 cups water, approximately
1 hen, cut into serving pieces
Salt and pepper to taste

1 cup okra, sliced in rounds
2/3 cup chopped parsley
1/2 cup chopped green onion tops
1/2 pound smoked sausage, cut into 6 pieces
1 pint fresh oysters

Heat oil in a heavy skillet. Gradually add flour, stirring constantly until a dark brown roux is formed. Stirring will take about 15 minutes. Do not let roux burn. Add chopped onion. Stir until wilted. Stir in water; blend well. Add chicken, salt, and pepper. Bring to a boil. Reduce heat; simmer for 30 minutes. Add okra, parsley, green onion tops, and sausage. Cook for 30 minutes. Add oysters. Simmer for 10 minutes more. Skim fat. Serve in bowls with a scoop of hot cooked white rice. Add a sprinkle of file' if desired. Serve with warm bread or crackers. Serves 6.

CORN AND SHRIMP SOUP

4 tablespoons corn oil
3 tablespoons flour
1 large onion, chopped
1 bell pepper, chopped
1 dozen ears fresh corn

1 clove garlic, minced
1 8-oz can tomato sauce
1½ pounds cleaned shrimp
3 quarts water, approximately
Salt and black pepper to taste

Heat oil in a large soup kettle. Add flour, stirring constantly until a light brown roux is formed. Add onion and bell pepper. Cook until wilted. Add balance of ingredients, except shrimp. (Cut corn off the cob before adding to mixture.) Bring to a boil, then reduce heat; simmer 40 minutes. Add shrimp; cook 15 minutes. Add more water if too thick. Serves 10.

DRIED SHRIMP GUMBO

½ cup corn oil
½ cup flour
10 cups water
1 small onion, chopped

2 3-oz. packages dried shrimp
½ cup chopped parsley
⅓ cup chopped green onion tops
⅛ teaspoon black pepper

Heat oil in a small, heavy skillet. Gradually add flour, stirring constantly until a dark brown roux is formed. Place roux in a large kettle. Add water, stirring to dissolve roux. Add chopped onion. Bring to a boil. Reduce heat; simmer for 20 minutes. Add shrimp, parsley, green onion tops, and black pepper. Simmer about 25 minutes, or until shrimp are plumped. Serve in bowls, with a scoop of hot cooked white rice. Garnish each bowl with a halved hard-boiled egg. Serve with soda crackers. Serves 6.

GUMBO d'HERBES

1 pound fresh mustard greens
½ pound fresh collards
1 can spinach, drained
6 tablespoons corn oil
4 tablespoons flour
1 medium onion, chopped

3 cloves garlic, chopped
6 cups water
¼ pound bacon, cut in half
¾ pound ham, cubed
Salt and pepper to taste

Wash fresh greens; pick off thick stems. Grind all vegetables together, except onion and garlic. Heat oil in a heavy pot. Gradually add flour, stirring constantly until a light brown roux is formed. Add onion and garlic; cook until wilted. Stir in water. Add balance of ingredients. Bring to a boil; reduce heat. Simmer for 1 hour. Discard bacon. Serve in bowls, with a scoop of hot cooked white rice. Serves 6.

This gumbo is often called green gumbo or grass gumbo. Other meats are often used in this gumbo—salt pork is most often used.

NAVY BEAN SOUP

½ pound dry navy beans
Water
2 tablespoons margarine
1 tablespoon flour
1 large onion, chopped
½ cup chopped bell pepper
2 cloves garlic, chopped

½ cup chopped celery
¼ cup chopped parsley
2 cups ripe tomatoes, chopped
Salt and black pepper to taste
¼ teaspoon Tabasco sauce
1 cup cubed ham

Place beans in large soup kettle; rinse well and drain. Cover beans with water and soak over night. Drain water and add 2 quarts fresh cold water. Heat margarine in sauce pan. Stir in flour; cook until golden. Add onion, bell pepper, and garlic; cook until wilted. Add to beans. Add balance of ingredients to beans. Bring to a boil, then reduce heat and simmer partially covered for about 1 hour, or until beans are tender. Heat and add more water if needed. Serves 8.

OYSTER SOUP

1 small onion, finely diced
¼ bell pepper, diced
2 stalks celery, finely diced
2 tablespoons butter
2 tablespoons margarine
3 dozen oysters with juice

1 tablespoon minced green
  onion tops
2 tablespoons minced parsley
1 quart milk, scalded
Salt and black pepper to taste

Stir and cook onion, bell pepper, and celery in butter and margarine until tender. Add oysters, including juice, and simmer 10 minutes. Add green onion tops and parsley. Simmer 5 minutes. Stir in milk. Season with salt and pepper to taste; simmer 1 minute. Serve with oyster crackers. Serves 4.

SEAFOOD GUMBO

2/3 cup corn oil
3/4 cup flour
1 large onion, chopped
1/4 bell pepper, chopped
1/4 cup chopped celery
2 quarts water
1 cup oyster juice
1/2 teaspoon salt

1/8 teaspoon fresh black pepper,
  or to taste
Pinch of ground red pepper
4 dozen raw oysters
1/2 pound fresh crab meat
1/2 cup chopped parsley
1/4 cup chopped green onion tops
2 1/2 pounds shrimp, cleaned

Heat corn oil in a heavy skillet. Gradually add flour, stirring constantly until a golden brown roux is formed. Add onion, bell pepper, and celery. Stir and cook until wilted. Place mixture into a large pot. Stir in water; blend well. Add oyster juice, salt, and peppers. Bring to a boil. Reduce heat; simmer for 20 minutes. Add balance of ingredients; simmer 20 minutes. Serve in bowls, with a scoop of hot cooked white rice. Serve with warm bread or crackers. Serves 6.

SHRIMP AND OKRA GUMBO

4 tablespoons corn oil
1 quart fresh okra, cut up
1 medium onion, chopped
½ bell pepper, chopped
3 fresh ripe tomatoes,
  peeled and diced

1 pound fresh shrimp,
  peeled and deveined
½ teaspoon salt, or to taste
¼ teaspoon black pepper
6 cups cold water

Heat oil in small skillet; stir and cook okra and onion until wilted. Place in a deep soup kettle. Add bell pepper and fresh tomatoes. Stir and cook 5 minutes. Add shrimp, salt, pepper, and water. Bring to a boil, then reduce heat; simmer 35 minutes. Serve with a scoop of hot cooked white rice in a soup bowl. Serves 4 to 6.

Most Cajuns and Creoles have their own version of gumbo—no two are alike, it seems. This shrimp gumbo was thickened with okra. No roux was used.

BAKED RED SNAPPER WITH STUFFING

1 medium onion, chopped
2 cloves garlic, minced
½ cup diced celery
4 tablespoons margarine
1 tablespoon minced parsley
½ cup chopped mushrooms
½ cup chopped fresh tomatoes
½ cup chopped cooked oysters
½ cup crabmeat, flaked
1 cup boiled shrimp, chopped
¼ teaspoon salt
⅛ teaspoon black pepper
Fine dried bread crumbs
1 egg, beaten
1 5-pound red snapper, dressed

Stir and cook onion, garlic, and celery in margarine until wilted. Mix together with balance of ingredients, except egg, using enough bread crumbs to make a medium-dry mixture. Add egg; mix well. Stuff fish lightly; secure with wood or metal skewers. Place fish into a greased baking dish. Season outside with additional salt and black pepper to taste. Baste often with melted margarine. Bake in a 350-degree oven for about 35 minutes, or until fish flakes. Serve with a flavored rice and crisp salad. Serves 6.

BLACKENED REDFISH

2 pounds fresh redfish, cut
  into six ½"-thick pieces
8 tablespoons butter, melted
½ teaspoon ground red pepper
½ teaspoon paprika
½ teaspoon white pepper
½ teaspoon black pepper
½ teaspoon onion powder
½ teaspoon garlic powder
½ teaspoon thyme, crushed
½ teaspoon basil, crushed
½ teaspoon salt

Heat a large iron skillet over high heat until a drop of water sizzles. Brush fish on both sides with some of the melted butter. Mix all seasonings in a bowl. Coat fish on both sides with seasonings. Put fish in hot skillet; put some of the butter over each piece of fish. Cook over high heat about 3 minutes. Turn fish over; pour remaining butter over fish. Cook for about 3 minutes, or until blackened. Vent for smoke! Serve with a flavored rice, or baked potato and a crisp green salad. Serves 6.

BUTTERFLY SHRIMP

3 dozen large fresh shrimp,
   cleaned
Salt to taste
Black pepper to taste
2 eggs, well-beaten

½ teaspoon salt
¼ cup whole milk
1½ cups flour
Corn oil

Slit shrimp on top almost all the way through; press to flatten a little. Season to taste with salt and pepper. In a small bowl, mix together beaten eggs, ½ teaspoon salt, and milk. Put flour in another small bowl. Coat shrimp with flour; shake off excess. Dip shrimp into egg mixture, then in flour—a thin coating is desired. Heat about 2 inches corn oil in skillet, or use a deep-fryer. Test one shrimp to see if oil is hot enough to start frying—shrimp should turn brown in less than 3 minutes. Drop shrimp into oil carefully, one at a time; fry about 12 at a time. Cook 3 to 4 minutes. Drain on paper towel. Serve with slaw, fries, and hush puppies. Serves. 4.

CAJUN SHRIMP SAUTE

1 cup celery, diagonally sliced
½ cup each, red and green bell
    pepper strips, thinly cut
1 cup thinly sliced mushrooms
½ cup chopped onion
2 tablespoons butter
1 tablespoon corn oil

1 14½-oz. can stewed
    tomatoes
1 teaspoon dried thyme
¼ teaspoon salt, or to taste
¼ teaspoon red pepper flakes
1 cup thinly sliced okra
1 cup cleaned fresh shrimp

In a large skillet saute' celery, bell pepper, mushrooms, and onion in butter and oil until wilted. Stir in tomatoes, including juice, thyme, salt, pepper, and okra. Bring to a boil. Reduce heat; simmer for 5 minutes, or until okra is just tender. Stir in shrimp; cook 7 minutes. Serve over hot cooked white rice. Serve with green salad and hot buttered rolls. Serves 4.

CATFISH CREOLE

3 tablespoons corn oil
1 medium onion, chopped
1 8-oz. can tomato sauce
1 cup water
2 tablespoons flour
1 3-pound catfish, cut into
  serving pieces

Salt to taste
Black pepper to taste
Ground red pepper to taste
½ cup chopped green onion tops
⅓ cup chopped parsley
2 cloves garlic, minced

Heat oil in dutch oven. Add onion and saute' until wilted. Add tomato sauce; cook 3 minutes, stirring constantly. Add water. Mix flour with small amount of water; stir into mixture. Season catfish with salt and peppers to taste. Add to mixture. Add balance of ingredients. Bring to a slow boil, then reduce heat and simmer for 35 minutes. Serve over hot cooked white rice. Serve with a green salad and French bread. Serves 6.

CORN MEAL FRIED OYSTERS

2 dozen large raw oysters
1 teaspoon salt
½ teaspoon black pepper
⅛ teaspoon cayenne pepper
2 egg yolks

½ cup cream
1 cup fine yellow corn meal
½ cup flour
½ teaspoon garlic powder
⅛ teaspoon salt

Season oysters with 1 teaspoon salt, black pepper, and cayenne pepper. In a small bowl, beat egg yolks with cream. In another bowl, combine corn meal, flour, garlic powder, and ⅛ teaspoon salt. Mix well. Dip oysters into egg mixture, then roll in corn meal mixture; coat well. Heat corn oil in a deep-fryer to 375 degrees. Fry oysters 2 to 3 minutes. Drain on paper towel. Serve with hush puppies and a creamy cole slaw. Serves 4.

CRAB MEAT AU GRATIN

1 medium onion, minced
½ cup minced celery
¼ cup butter
½ cup flour
1 5-oz. can evaporated milk

2 egg yolks, beaten
Salt and black pepper to taste
1 pound lump crab meat
½ pound Cheddar cheese,
    grated

Stir and cook onion and celery in butter until tender. Stir in flour, blending well. Stir in milk. Quickly stir in egg yolks. Add salt, pepper, and crab meat. Blend well. Put mixture into a greased oblong glass casserole. Top with cheese. Bake in a 375-degree oven for about 15 minutes, or until light-golden on top. Serve with a crisp saland and French bread. Serves 4.

CRAB MEAT ETOUFFEE

6 tablespoons corn oil
2 tablespoons flour
1 medium onion, minced
½ cup finely diced celery
½ cup diced bell pepper
1 pound crab meat

2 tablespoons chopped parsley
2 tablespoons chopped green
  onion tops
3 tablespoons water
Salt and black pepper to taste

Heat oil in a medium saucepan. Gradually add flour, stirring constantly until brown. Add onion, celery, and bell pepper. Cook and stir until wilted. Add balance of ingredients. Bring to a boil, then reduce heat; simmer 20 minutes. Serve over hot cooked white rice. Serve with sliced tomatoes and cucumber spears. Serves 4.

CRAWFISH ETOUFFEE

8 tablespoons butter
1 small onion, chopped
½ cup chopped green onion tops
Crawfish fat, as desired

1 pound cleaned crawfish tails
Salt and red pepper to taste
¼ cup minced parsley
Red pepper sauce

Heat butter in saucepan. Stir-fry chopped onion and green onion tops until wilted. Add crawfish fat; cover and cook for 5 minutes. Add crawfish tails; season with salt and ground red pepper to taste. Cover and cook 15 minutes more. Stir in parsley just before serving. Season with red pepper sauce as desired. Serve over white cooked rice. Serve with crisp salad and warm bread. Serves 4.

CRAWFISH PIE

6 tablespoons margarine
4 tablespoons flour
1 large onion, finely chopped
½ cup diced celery
½ cup chopped bell pepper
2 cloves garlic, minced
½ cup tomato sauce

2 cups water
1 pound cleaned crawfish tails
⅓ cup minced parsley
⅓ cup minced green onion tops
Salt to taste
Black pepper to taste
⅛ teaspoon ground red pepper

Heat margarine in saucepan. Add flour, stirring constantly until a light brown roux is formed. Add onion, celery, and garlic. Stir and cook until wilted. Add tomato sauce and water. Bring to a boil, then reduce heat. Simmer 15 minutes. Add balance of ingredients. Simmer 15 minutes more. Line a 9-inch pie pan with pie crust. Pour in cooled mixture. Top with pie crust; seal edges, and make 3 slits on top. Bake in a preheated 450-degree oven for 10 minutes. Reduce heat to 375 degrees. Bake for 35 minutes, or until crust is golden. Makes 1 pie.

CRAWFISH STEW

4 tablespoons corn oil
1 medium onion, chopped
½ cup chopped bell pepper
½ cup chopped celery
3 tablespoons flour

2 cups fish stock or water
1 pound cleaned crawfish tails
½ teaspoon salt
⅛ teaspoon black pepper
⅛ teaspoon red pepper

Heat oil in heavy saucepan. Add onion, bell pepper, and celery. Stir and cook until wilted; remove and set aside. Add flour to same oil, and cook stirring constantly until a light brown roux is formed. Stir in fish stock or water. Return vegetables to pan. Add crawfish tails and seasonings. Bring to a boil, then reduce heat; simmer for 20 minutes. Serve over hot cooked white rice. Serve with green salad tossed with a vinegar and oil dressing. Serves 4.

PO' BOYS

2 eggs, well-beaten
½ cup light cream
½ teaspoon salt
¼ teaspoon black pepper
1 cup dry fine bread crumbs
1 tablespoon flour

2 dozen fresh oysters
Corn oil for deep frying
1 loaf unsliced French bread,
    cut horizontally
Dill pickles, shredded lettuce
Tabasco sauce

Mix eggs, cream, salt, and black pepper in a small bowl. Combine bread crumbs and flour in another small bowl. Dip oysters into egg mixture, then roll in bread crumbs. Heat enough corn oil for deep-frying in a heavy skillet, or use a deep-fryer. Fry a few oysters at a time for about 2 minutes. Drain on paper towel. Scoop out a little of the inside of the bread and discard. Heat the bread; spread with butter and mayonnaise on inside top and bottom. Put oysters on bottom; top with pickle, lettuce, and a few drops of Tabasco sauce. Add top to complete loaf. Slice and serve warm. Serves 4.

REDFISH COURTBOUILLON

5 tablespoons corn oil
4 tablespoons flour
1 large onion, chopped
½ cup chopped bell pepper
½ cup chopped celery
3 cloves garlic, minced
1 8-oz. can tomato sauce
1 16-oz. can whole tomatoes, chopped

2 teaspoons Worchestershire
2 cups water
1 thin slice of lemon
¼ cup chopped parsley
1 teaspoon salt, or to taste
¼ teaspoon ground red pepper
½ cup white wine
3 pounds redfish, cut into serving pieces

Heat corn oil in heavy dutch oven. Gradually add flour, stirring constantly for 10 minutes. Add chopped onion and cook until wilted. Add balance of ingredients, except wine and fish. Bring to a boil; reduce heat and simmer 25 minutes. Add wine and redfish. Bring to a slow boil; reduce heat and simmer about 25 minutes. Serve over hot cooked white rice. Serve with fresh green beans, green salad, and hard rolls. Serves 6.

SALMON IN SAUCE

1 medium onion, chopped
¼ bell pepper, chopped
2 cloves garlic, chopped
2 tablespoons corn oil
2 tablespoons flour
2 cups water
1 7-oz. can tomato sauce
¼ cup chopped parsley
¼ cup chopped green onion tops
1 16-oz. can salmon, drained
Salt and pepper to taste

In a medium saucepan, saute' onion, bell pepper, and garlic in corn oil until wilted. Stir in flour, blending well. Add water, stirring constantly to make a smooth, thin sauce. Add balance of ingredients, except salmon. Bring to a boil. Reduce heat; simmer for 20 minutes. Add salmon; simmer gently for 10 minutes—try to keep the salmon in solid pieces. Serve over hot cooked white rice. Serve with crisp green salad. Serves 4.

SHRIMP BOULETTES

1 pound chopped shrimp
1/8 teaspoon black pepper
1/2 teaspoon salt, or to taste
1 tablespoon minced onion
2 cloves garlic, minced
1/3 cup minced green onion tops

1/8 teaspoon ground red pepper
1 egg, well-beaten
2 tablespoons milk
1/2 cup fine dry bread crumbs
Corn oil for frying

In a large bowl, season shrimp with pepper and salt. Add balance of ingredients, except corn oil; mix well. Form into boulettes (balls), using 1 tablespoonful for each ball. Coat boulettes with additional fine dry bread crumbs. Heat corn oil in a heavy skillet, or use a deep-fryer. Fry a few boulettes at a time for 1 to 2 minutes, or until done. Remove with slotted spoon; drain on paper towel. Serve with a creamy cole slaw. Serves 4.

SHRIMP CREOLE

4 tablespoon corn oil
1 medium onion, chopped
1/2 cup bell pepper, chopped
1/2 cup chopped celery
2 cloves garlic, chopped
1 8-oz. can tomato sauce
2 cups water
1/2 cup chopped green onion tops

1/2 cup chopped parsley
3/4 teaspoon salt
1/4 teaspoon black pepper
1/8 teaspoon red pepper
2 tablespoons flour
1 bay leaf (optional)
2 pounds fresh raw shrimp, deveined

Heat oil in a large skillet. Stir and cook onion, bell pepper, celery, and garlic until wilted. Add tomato sauce; cook 3 minutes, stirring constantly. Add water; bring to a boil. Reduce heat. Add green onion tops, parsley, and seasonings; simmer 30 minutes. Mix flour with a little water; stir into sauce. Add bay leaf and shrimp; cook 15 minutes. Discard bay leaf. A thin sauce is desired. Add water if needed. Serve over hot cooked white rice. Serve with green salad and French bread. Serves 4.

SHRIMP ETOUFFEE

6 tablespoons margarine
1 cup chopped onion
½ cup chopped celery
½ cup chopped bell pepper
3 cloves garlic, chopped
2 tablespoons flour

1 tablespoon tomato paste
2 pounds peeled shrimp
Salt, black and red pepper
1 cup water, approximately
¼ cup chopped parsley
¼ cup chopped green onion tops

Heat margarine in skillet. Add onion, celery, bell pepper, and garlic. Stir and cook until tender. Add flour; stir until light brown. Stir in tomato paste; cook 1 minute, stirring constantly. Add shrimp. Season with salt, black pepper, and red pepper to taste. Bring to a boil, then reduce heat; simmer about 20 minutes. Add parsley and green onion tops. Cook 3 minutes. Serve over hot cooked white rice. Serve with a shredded cabbage salad. Serves 4 to 6.

SHRIMP JAMBALAYA

3 tablespoons margarine
1 medium onion, chopped
½ cup chopped bell pepper
¾ cup chopped celery
2 cloves garlic, chopped
1 16-oz. can stewed tomatoes
¾ cup tomato paste

Salt to taste
Black and ground red pepper
1½ cups boiled shrimp,
    deveined
1½ cups cooked ham, cubed
¼ cup chopped green onion tops
2 cups cooked white rice

Heat margarine in a large heavy saucepan. Stir and cook onion, bell pepper, celery, and garlic until wilted. Add tomatoes and tomato paste. Season to taste with salt, black pepper, and ground red pepper; stir well. Cover and bring to a boil. Reduce heat; simmer for 20 minutes. Add shrimp, ham, green onion tops, and rice. Toss mixture over low heat until hot. Serve with boiled okra, drizzled with white vinegar, and a crisp green salad. Serves 4 to 6.

SHRIMP SALAD

1 pound boiled shrimp,
  deveined and cut in half
3 stalks celery, finely diced
3 hard-boiled eggs, chopped
1 tablespoon chopped
  sweet pickle
1 teaspoon prepared mustard

1 cup mayonnaise
1 teaspoon salt
1/8 teaspoon black pepper
Pinch of ground red pepper
1 tablespoon grated onion
1 teaspoon Worcestershire sauce

Combine ingredients; blend well. Serve chilled on a bed of shredded lettuce in salad bowls. Garnish with fresh tomato wedges. Serve with crisp crackers. Serves 4.

STUFFED CRABS

1 cup chopped onions
½ cup chopped bell pepper
½ cup chopped celery
8 tablespoons butter
1 pound fresh crab meat
6 slices bread, toasted
1 cup evaporated milk
½ teaspoon Worcestershire
3 eggs, slightly beaten
Salt and pepper to taste
Ground red pepper to taste
1 tablespoon minced parsley
½ cup minced green onion tops
Dry bread crumbs

Stir and cook onion, bell pepper, and celery in butter until tender. Add crab meat; cook 5 minutes. Soak toasted bread in milk; squeeze milk out; add bread and remaining milk to crab mixture. Add balance of ingredients, except dry bread crumbs; mix well. Put into 12 clean crab shells, or use individual casseroles. Top with dry bread crumbs. Dot with additional butter. Bake in 375-degree oven for 15 minutes, or until piping hot. Serve with torn lettuce salad, fresh sliced tomatoes, and hot rolls. Serves 6.

CHICKEN FRICASSEE

6 tablespoons corn oil
1 4-pound fresh hen,
   cut into serving pieces
6 tablespoons flour
1 large onion, chopped

4 cups hot water
½ cup chopped parsley
½ cup chopped green onion tops
2 cloves garlic, chopped
Salt and black pepper to taste

Heat oil in a heavy pot. Add chicken; brown and set aside. Gradually add flour to pot, stirring constantly until a dark brown roux is formed, about 15 minutes. Add chopped onion; stir and cook until soft. Add water, parsley, green onion tops, and garlic. Season to taste with salt and pepper. Return chicken to pot. Bring to a slow boil. Reduce heat and simmer for 40 minutes, or until chicken is tender. A thick gravy is desired. Serve over hot white rice. Serve with baked sweet potatoes, green cabbage salad, and buttered corn bread. Serves 6.

CHICKEN SAUCE PIQUANTE

3 tablespoons corn oil
1 3-pound chicken, cut into
  serving pieces
Salt, red pepper, black pepper
½ pound smoked sausage, cut
  into 6 pieces
1 large onion, chopped
½ bell pepper, chopped
3 cloves garlic, chopped
½ cup chopped celery
1 8-oz. can tomato sauce
1 small can button mushrooms
½ cup red wine
2 cups water, approximately

Heat oil in heavy dutch oven. Season chicken with salt, ground red pepper, and black pepper to taste; brown in oil and remove from pot. Brown sausage for 5 minutes and remove from pot. Add onion, bell pepper, garlic, and celery; stir until wilted. Add tomato sauce, stir and cook for 5 minutes. Return chicken and sausage to pot. Add balance of ingredients. Bring to a boil, then reduce heat; cover and simmer for about 1 hour. Check often; add water if needed. Serve with cooked rice. Serve with green salad and fresh sliced cantaloupe. Serves 6.

CHICKEN-SHRIMP ETOUFFEE

¼ cup corn oil
6 chicken thighs, boned
2 chicken breast, cut in half
4 tablespoons butter
6 tablespoons flour
2 medium onions, chopped
1 bell pepper, chopped
4 cloves garlic, chopped
1 cup chopped celery
1 6-oz. can tomato paste
4 cups chicken stock or water
¼ teaspoon dried thyme
Salt and pepper to taste
½ cup chopped parsley
2 pounds cleaned shrimp

Heat oil in large skillet. Brown chicken; remove. Add butter to same skillet. Add flour, stirring constantly for 15 minutes, or until a medium brown roux is formed. Add onions, bell pepper, garlic, and celery. Stir and cook until wilted. Add tomato paste; stir for 3 minutes. Add stock; blend well. Return chicken to skillet. Add thyme, salt, pepper to taste, and parsley. Bring to a boil. Reduce heat; simmer 35 minutes. Add shrimp; cook 20 minutes. Serve over hot cooked white rice. Serve with green salad and French bread. Serves 10.

CHICKEN-TASSO JAMBALAYA

1/4 cup corn oil
1 pound boned chicken
  meat, cut bite-size
1 tablespoon margarine
1 large onion, chopped
1/2 bell pepper, chopped
3 stalks celery, chopped
3 cloves garlic, chopped
1/3 cup water

2 cups canned tomatoes
  in juice, chopped
1/2 small can tomato paste
1 small piece tasso, diced
1/4 teaspoon salt
1/8 teaspoon black pepper
Pinch of ground red pepper
2 1/2 cups cooked white rice

Heat oil in a large pot. Add chicken; stir and cook for 10 minutes; remove. Add margarine to pot; stir and cook raw vegetables until wilted. Add water, tomatoes, and tomato paste. Stir well. Return chicken to pot. Stir in seasonings and tasso. Bring to a boil. Reduce heat; cover; simmer for 40 minutes. When cooked, add rice. Toss and heat throughly. Serve with a crisp green salad and warm bread. Serves 4 to 6.

Use ham or smoked sausage if tasso is not available.

SMOTHERED CHICKEN BREAST

3 tablespoons corn oil
Salt and black pepper to taste
4 chicken breasts, skin removed

1 large onion, chopped
4 cloves garlic, chopped
Water

Heat oil in heavy skillet over medium heat. Add seasoned chicken, chopped onion, and garlic. Stir and cook, browning chicken on all sides. Add ½ cup water. Cover with lid partially off the skillet, to allow some steam to escape. Check often. When water is reduced to oil, turn chicken over and add ½ cup more water. Cover as before and continue same process of reducing to oil and adding water for 1 hour. Uncover and let water reduce to oil, turn chicken over once in oil, then remove to warm platter. Add ¾ cup water to drippings, stirring well to scrape the bottom and sides of skillet. Simmer for 3 minutes. Serve this natural sauce over hot cooked white rice along with chicken. Serve with maque choux (page 76) and a green salad. Serves 4.

CREOLE MEAT LOAF

½ cup chopped onion
½ cup chopped celery
¼ cup chopped bell pepper
2 tablespoons margarine
1½ cups ketchup

1½ pounds ground beef
1 cup soft bread crumbs
1 egg, slightly beaten
½ teaspoon salt, or to taste
⅛ teaspoon black pepper

Stir and cook onion, celery, and bell pepper in margarine until tender. Stir in ketchup. Combine ½ cup plus 3 tablespoons of mixture with ground beef, bread crumbs, egg, salt, and pepper. Mix well. Form into a loaf. Put into an 8x4-inch shallow baking pan. Bake in preheated oven at 350 degrees for 1 hour. Simmer remaining sauce in small pan over low heat for 15 minutes—add a little water if needed. When meat loaf is cooked, take out of oven and let rest a few minutes before slicing. Top each serving with warm sauce. Serve with creamed potatoes, green beans, and a crisp salad. Serves 6.

SHORT RIBS PIQUANTE

3 tablespoons corn oil
3 pounds beef short ribs
Salt and black pepper to taste
Cayenne pepper to taste
1 large onion, chopped
½ bell pepper, diced

3 cloves garlic, chopped
1 8-oz. can tomato sauce
3 tablespoons flour
2 fresh tomatoes, chopped
½ cup chopped green onion tops
4 cups water

Heat oil in dutch oven. Season ribs with salt, black pepper, and cayenne pepper to taste. Brown in oil; remove. Add onion, bell pepper, and garlic; stir and cook until wilted. Add tomato sauce; stir 3 minutes. Dissolve flour in a little water; add to mixture, blending well. Return ribs to dutch oven. Add balance of ingredients. Bring to a boil; reduce heat; cover and cook over medium heat for 1½ hours, or until ribs are tender. Add more water if needed. Serve over hot cooked white rice. Serve with mustard greens and wilted cucumbers. Serves 6.

SMOTHERED LIVER AND ONIONS

2 pounds calf liver
½ teaspoon salt
¼ teaspoon black pepper
½ cup flour
4 tablespoons corn oil

2 medium onions, chopped
3 cloves garlic, chopped
2 green onions, tops and
bottoms, chopped
1 cup water

Cut liver into serving pieces. Season with salt and black pepper. Coat liver with flour. Heat oil in heavy skillet. Add liver and fry quickly, browning both sides. Add onions and garlic; stir and cook until light brown. Add green onions and 1 cup water. Bring to a boil; reduce heat; simmer 30 minutes, or until liver tests done. Serve over hot cooked white rice. Serve with buttered white corn and fresh sliced tomatoes. Serves 6.

STEAK AND GRAVY

2 pounds top sirloin steak
Salt and black pepper to taste
3 tablespoons corn oil

1 medium onion, chopped
3 cloves garlic, chopped
Water

Cut meat into 3x5-inch pieces. Season with salt and pepper. Heat oil in heavy skillet. Add meat, onion and garlic. Stir and cook, browning meat on both sides. Add ½ cup water. Cover with lid partially off, allowing some steam to escape. When water is reduced to oil, add ½ cup more water; cover as before. Continue this process for 1 hour. Then uncover completely. Reduce to oil; turn meat over once in oil and remove to serving platter. Add ¾ cup water; simmer 3 minutes. Serve the natural sauce over hot cooked white rice along with meat. Serve with a lettuce and tomato salad and smothered okra (page 78). Serves 4 to 6.

TONGUE SALAD

1 small green cabbage	1 sweet red pepper, chopped
1 cup cooked cold tongue, diced	½ cup chopped onion
1 cup cooked cold ham, diced	1 cup mayonnaise
1 bell pepper, chopped	Salt and pepper to taste

Shred the cabbage very fine. Place in a large bowl with balance of ingredients; mix well. Garnish with banana peppers and cherry tomatoes. Serve with bread sticks and crackers. Serves 4 to 6.

DRIED BLACKEYED PEAS JAMBALAYA

½ pound dried blackeyed peas
2 tablespoons margarine
1 small onion, minced
1 quart water
¾ cup diced ham

Salt to taste
Black pepper to taste
½ cup chopped parsley
½ cup chopped green onion tops
2 cups cooked white rice

Rinse blackeyed peas; drain. Add 1 quart water; let soak for 10 minutes. Add balance of ingredients, except parsley, green onion tops, and cooked rice. Bring to a boil; reduce heat; simmer until peas are tender, about 35 minutes. Consistency should be creamy, but not too much water. When cooked, add parsley, green onion tops, and rice. Mix well. Serve hot. Serve with cabbage salad dressed with vinegar and oil, fresh sliced tomatoes, and hard rolls. Serves 4.

PORK CHOPS

4 tablespoons corn oil
Salt and pepper to taste
4 large pork chops

1 large onion, chopped
3 large cloves garlic, chopped
Water

Heat oil in large skillet. Add seasoned pork chops, onion, and garlic. Brown pork chops on both sides. Saute' onion and garlic with the pork chops until light brown. Add ½ cup water; bring to a boil; reduce heat. Cook partially-covered until water is reduced to oil. Turn pork chops over. Add ½ cup water. Cover as before and continue the process of reducing to oil, adding ½ cup water, for 1 hour. Remove cover and let water reduce completely. Turn pork chops over once, then remove to a warm platter. Add 1 cup water to drippings. Scrape to deglaze. Simmer a few minutes. Serve natural sauce over hot cooked rice. Serve with buttered corn and crisp salad. Serves 4.

PORK GRILLADES

1½ pounds pork tenderloin, cut into 3-inch thin strips
Salt and black pepper to taste
3 tablespoons corn oil
Flour
1 large onion, chopped
½ cup chopped green onion tops
½ cup diced celery
3 cloves garlic, chopped
1 16-oz. can tomatoes, chopped
Dash of cayenne pepper
½ cup water, approximately

Season pork with salt and pepper. In a heavy skillet, heat oil to piping hot. Roll pork in flour; shake off excess. Brown pork on both sides, turning only once; remove. Add onion to skillet; stir and cook until wilted. Add balance of ingredients. Stir well. Return pork to skillet. Bring to a boil, then reduce heat. Cover and simmer about 30 minutes, or until meat is tender. Serve over hot cooked grits or rice. Serves 4.

To most Cajuns, "grillades" means getting a small piece of meat, whether it's beef or pork. There are various methods of preparing grillades—plain or with sauces, marinated, etc.

PORK ROAST

1 6-pound pork roast
2 cloves garlic, slivered
2 tablespoons slivered onion
1 tablespoon slivered green
bell pepper

1 teaspoon salt, or to taste
½ teaspoon black pepper
¼ teaspoon ground red pepper
2 tablespoons corn oil

Remove excess fat from roast and discard. Make slits in meat, covering the whole roast. Fill slits with slivered vegetables; press slit to secure firmly. Season meat wtih salt and peppers. Place oil in dutch oven; add meat. Roast partially-covered in 350-degree oven for about 2½ hours, or until meat tests done. Add a little water during cooking period. Remove meat to platter. Add ⅔ cup water to drippings; simmer on top of stove until well-blended. Serve natural sauce over hot cooked white rice. Serve with black-eyed peas and cabbage salad with a vinegar dressing. Serves 10.

RED BEANS AND RICE

½ pound dried red beans
¾ pound ham, coarsely cut
1 large onion, chopped
3 stalks celery, chopped
½ green bell pepper, chopped
5 tablespoons chopped parsley

3 cloves garlic, minced
1 tablespoon Worcestershire sauce, or to taste
Salt and pepper to taste
Water

Wash and pick beans well; drain. Place beans in a large soup kettle; cover with cold water; soak overnight. Drain beans; cover with fresh cold water. Add all ingredients, except Worcestershire sauce and black pepper. Bring to a boil; reduce heat; simmer for about 2 hours, or until beans are tender. Add more water as needed. Add Worcestershire sauce and black pepper; simmer a little longer. Serve over hot cooked white rice. Serve with a crisp green salad and French bread. Serves 6.

For a creamier consistency, stir in 2 tablespoons margarine just before beans are done.

ALLIGATOR SAUCE PIQUANTE

½ cup corn oil
6 tablespoons flour
1 large onion, chopped
2 cloves garlic, minced
½ cup chopped bell pepper
2 cups canned tomatoes

1 8-oz. can tomato sauce
1½ pounds alligator meat, cut
    into bite-size pieces
½ cup chopped green onion tops
3 cups water or fish stock
Salt, red and black pepper

Heat oil in large pot. Gradually add flour; stir constantly until a brown roux is formed. Add onion, garlic, and bell pepper; cook until wilted. Add balance of ingredients, seasoning with salt, red pepper, and black pepper to taste. Bring to a boil; reduce heat; cook about 45 minutes, or until meat is tender. Serve over hot cooked rice. Serves 6.

BAKED WILD DUCKS

2 wild ducks, dressed
Salt, red and black pepper
1 medium onion, halved
2 stalks celery, halved
1 medium onion, chopped
¼ cup corn oil

1¼ cups water or chicken stock
1 cup sherry wine
1 tablespoon flour
½ cup water
2 tablespoons chopped parsley

Season ducks inside and out with salt and peppers to taste. Put onion and celery into cavity of each duck. Heat oil in heavy dutch oven; brown ducks. Add chopped onion; stir and cook until wilted. Add 1 cup water and wine. Cover and cook in 350-degree oven for about 2 hours, or until meat tests done. Baste often. Add more water if needed. When cooked, remove ducks to platter. Mix flour with small amount of water; stir into drippings to make a smooth, thin gravy. Stir in parsley. Serve gravy over hot cooked rice along with duck. Serves 8.

DEEP-FRIED ALLIGATOR

3 lemons, juiced
1 small bottle Tabasco sauce
½ teaspoon salt
⅛ teaspoon black pepper
Water

2 pounds alligator tail meat,
  cut into serving pieces
Salt and ground red pepper
Cornmeal and flour, mixed
Corn oil

Combine lemon juice, Tabasco, ½ teaspoon salt, black pepper; and enough water to cover meat. Place meat into a large glass bowl, and cover with marinade. Marinate in refrigerator 24 to 48 hours. Drain well. Season with salt and ground red pepper to taste. Roll meat in cornmeal and flour mixture. Heat enough corn oil in a heavy pot to deep-fry. Fry alligator until golden brown. Serve with cole slaw, hot banana peppers, dirty rice (page 83), and hot hush puppies. Serves 6.

FRIED SQUIRREL

6 tablespoons corn oil
2 squirrels, dressed and cut
   into serving pieces

Salt and black pepper to taste
2 medium onions, chopped
Water

Heat corn oil in a large skillet. Season the meat with salt and pepper; brown well. Add onions; stir and cook until brown. Add ½ cup water; stir well. Bring to a boil; reduce heat; simmer for 1 hour, or until meat tests done. Check often, adding ½ cup water as needed. When meat is done, let water reduce to oil. Turn meat over once in oil, then remove to platter. Add enough water to drippings to serve as a sauce; simmer 3 minutes. Serve over hot cooked white rice along with a wilted lettuce salad. Serves 4

RABBIT STEW

1 large rabbit, dressed
6 tablespoons corn oil
2 medium onions, chopped
3 cloves garlic, chopped
½ cup tomato paste
3 large fresh tomatoes,
  peeled and chopped

1 cup water
Tabasco sauce to taste
Salt and black pepper to taste
1 cup canned sliced mushrooms
½ cup chopped parsley
¼ cup chopped green onion tops

Cut rabbit into serving pieces; brown in heated oil; remove. Stir and cook onions and garlic until wilted in same skillet. Add tomato paste; cook 5 minutes, stirring constantly. Add fresh tomatoes and 1 cup water; stir well. Cook 20 minutes. Add rabbit, Tabasco sauce, salt and black pepper to taste. Cook for about 1 hour. Add mushrooms, parsley, and green onion tops just before cooking period is up. Serve over white cooked rice. Serves 6.

SMOTHERED QUAIL

3 slices bacon
2 tablespoons corn oil
6 quails
Salt and pepper to taste

4 tablespoons flour
1 medium onion, chopped
2 cups chicken broth or water
1 tablespoon chopped parsley

Fry bacon in skillet until crisp; remove and set aside. Add oil to skillet. Season quails with salt and pepper to taste; brown and set aside. Add flour to skillet; blend well. Add onion; stir fry until wilted. Return bacon and quails to skillet. Add balance of ingredients. Bring to a boil; reduce heat; simmer for 30 minutes, or until meat is tender. Serve natural sauce over hot white rice. Serve with buttered corn and lettuce salad. Serves 6.

TEAL JAMBALAYA

3 tablespoons corn oil
2 medium onions, chopped
3 teals, cut into serving pieces
3 cloves garlic, chopped
1/4 cup chopped green onion tops

2 tablespoons chopped parsley
2½ cups water
1½ cups white rice, raw
Tabasco sauce to taste
Salt and pepper to taste

Heat oil in skillet; stir and cook onions until brown. Add meat; brown. Add garlic; stir-fry lightly. Add balance of ingredients, except rice; simmer about 45 minutes. Add rice; cook 25 minutes; add more water if needed. Rice should be done, but not too soft. Serve with a garnish tray of fresh tomatoes, cucumber spears, radishes, and sweet peppers. Serves 6.

TURTLE SAUCE PIQUANTE

½ cup corn oil
3 pounds turtle meat, cut
  into serving pieces
2 large onions, chopped
½ cup chopped bell pepper
3 cloves garlic, minced

⅔ cup chopped celery
1 small can sliced mushrooms
1 cup tomato paste
2 cups water
Salt to taste
Black and red pepper to taste

Heat oil in large saucepan. Add turtle meat; stir and cook until brown; remove. Add onions, bell pepper, garlic, and celery to the saucepan; cook until transparent. Return meat to saucepan. Add balance of ingredients. Cook over medium heat until tender, about 1 hour. Stir often. Serve over hot cooked white rice. Serves 8.

TURTLE SOUP

4 tablespoons corn oil
3 pounds turtle meat, diced
4 tablespoons flour
1 cup chopped onion
½ bell pepper, chopped
1 cup sliced celery
3 cloves garlic, chopped
¼ cup chopped parsley

1 8-oz. can tomato sauce
2 teaspoons Worcestershire sauce
1 tablespoon fresh lemon juice
½ cup apple cider
⅛ teaspoon thyme
Dash Tabasco sauce
Salt and pepper to taste

Heat corn oil in a heavy pot. Add meat. Stir and cook until slightly brown; remove. Add flour to pot, stirring until a light brown roux is formed. Add onion, bell pepper, celery, and garlic. Cook until wilted. Add balance of ingredients and about 10 cups water. Bring to a boil. Reduce heat and simmer until meat is tender, about 1 hour. Serves 6.

BAKED SWEET POTATOES

Wash and dry sweet potatoes. Preheat oven to 350 degrees. Bake potatoes about 1 hour, depending on size, until soft to touch. Remove from oven and let stand a minute. To serve warm, peel jackets right away. Split open, and add a little butter or margarine. May be served plain, warm or cold. Delicious in a bowl topped with milk or cream. Great with pork stew or chicken fricassee.

BEET AND POTATO SALAD

3 medium potatoes, boiled
3 beets, boiled
3 eggs, hard boiled
½ teaspoon sugar

4 slices bacon
1 small onion, thinly sliced
1 tablespoon white vinegar
Salt and black pepper to taste

In a medium bowl, slice potatoes. Remove skin from beets and slice; add to bowl. Add sliced eggs. Sprinkle with sugar. Fry bacon in a small skillet; remove and crumble into potato mixture. Drain most of bacon fat; add onion to skillet; stir in vinegar. Pour over potato mixture. Season to taste. Toss until well-coated. Serve warm. Serves 6.

CANDIED YAMS

8 medium yams, boiled
   and peeled
¾ cup brown sugar
¾ cup white sugar
4 tablespoons water

½ teaspoon cinnamon
⅛ teaspoon nutmeg
1 teaspoon vanilla
4 tablespoons margarine
½ cup toasted chopped pecans

Put cooked yams in a buttered glass casserole. In a saucepan, mix together sugars and water; bring to a boil. Stir in cinnamon, nutmeg, vanilla, and margarine. Pour over yams. Bake in a 350-degree oven about 20 minutes, or until syrup is to desired thickness. Spoon syrup over yams several times. Top with toasted pecans. Serves 8.

COLE SLAW ACADIANA

3 cups shredded green cabbage
2 carrots, grated
2 tablespoons minced onion
1 small bell pepper, diced
½ cup finely diced celery

½ cup radishes, finely chopped
½ cup mayonnaise
1 tablespoon sugar
1 tablespoon vinegar
Salt and pepper to taste

Combine all ingredients in a large bowl. Mix until well-blended. Add more mayonnaise if needed. Chill before serving. Refrigerate. Serves 6.

CREOLE SWEET POTATOES

8 baked sweet potatoes
1 lemon, sliced—discard rind
3 oranges, peeled and sliced
1⅓ cups crushed pineapple
2¼ cups pineapple juice

1 cup brown sugar
½ teaspoon salt
1 teaspoon vanilla
5 tablespoons butter

Peel sweet potatoes; cut into 4 lengthwise strips. Place alternate layers of potatoes, sliced lemon, sliced oranges, and pineapple in a buttered glass casserole. Combine balance of ingredients in a saucepan; cook to a thick syrup. Pour syrup over potatoes. Bake in preheated 350-degree oven for about 40 minutes. Serves 8.

FRESH BUTTER BEANS

1 tablespoon corn oil	2 slices bacon
2 teaspoons flour	1/4 teaspoon salt
2 tablespoons diced onion	Black pepper to taste
1/2 pound fresh butter beans	2 cups water

Heat oil in medium saucepan. Add flour; stir constantly until light brown, about 3 minutes. Add onion and butter beans; stir until onion is tender. Add bacon, salt, black pepper, and water. Bring to a boil; reduce heat; simmer until butter beans are tender. Heat and add more water if needed. Discard bacon. Serve as a side dish over hot cooked rice. Serves 4.

MAQUE CHOUX

4 tablespoons butter
2 tablespoons corn oil
1 large onion, chopped
½ cup diced bell pepper

12 ears fresh sweet corn
2 very ripe fresh tomatoes,
    peeled and chopped
Salt and black pepper to taste

In a heavy dutch oven, heat butter and oil. Saute' onion and bell pepper until wilted. Cut the corn off the cob; scrape the cob to get all the milk; add to corn. Add corn to dutch oven. Cook covered about 10 minutes, stirring often. Add tomatoes, salt and black pepper to taste. Cook 10 minutes. Add a little milk if sticking. Serves 6.

Maque Choux is one of the earlier Creole dishes—delicious and simple to prepare. Serve over rice with natural juice gravy, along with pork roast or other meat dishes.

MUSTARD GREENS

1 pound fresh mustard greens   ½ teaspoon salt
Water   4 slices bacon, cut in half

Wash greens; pick off the heavy stems and discard. Place greens in saucepan; add enough water to cover. Add salt and bacon. Bring to a boil. Reduce heat; cook about 35 minutes, or until greens are tender. Discard bacon. Drain well; coarsely chop in saucepan. Butter the greens or drizzle with a seasoned vinegar. Serves 4.

SMOTHERED OKRA

2 pounds fresh okra
3 tablespoons corn oil
2 tablespoons corn oil
1 tablespoon flour
1/4 bell pepper, diced

1 medium onion, chopped
3 large ripe fresh tomatoes, peeled and chopped, or use 1 can whole tomatoes
Salt and black pepper to taste

Wash and dry fresh okra. Cut into thin round slices. Add enough oil in a large skillet (do not use cast iron skillet) to cover bottom, about 3 tablespoons. Stir and cook okra for 15 minutes—do not let burn. In another skillet, heat 2 tablespoons corn oil; gradually add flour, stirring constantly until a light brown roux is formed. Add bell pepper and onion; stir until wilted. Add tomatoes, salt and pepper. Stir in cooked okra. Simmer for 30 minutes over low heat. Check and stir often. Add water if sticking. Serve over rice, along with meat dishes using natural juice sauce. Serves 4 to 6.

SWEET POTATO SOUFFLE

1 cup milk
½ cup sugar
½ teaspoon salt
3 tablespoons butter
1 teaspoon nutmeg, scant
1½ teaspoons vanilla

2 cups sweet potatoes, mashed
2 eggs, separated
½ cup chopped pecans
½ cup raisins
Marshmallows

Scald milk in a saucepan. Add sugar, salt, butter, nutmeg, vanilla, and sweet potatoes. Beat egg yolks; add to potato mixture, stirring fast. Add pecans and raisins. Beat egg whites until stiff; fold into mixture. Pour mixture into a greased glass baking dish. Bake in a 350-degree oven for 1 hour, or until firm. Top with marshmallows; brown lightly. Serves 8.

ZUCCHINI AND OKRA

2 tablespoons corn oil
2 small zucchini, cut in large chunks
¼ green bell pepper, chopped
1 small onion, chopped

1 clove garlic, chopped
½ cup sliced raw okra
2 fresh ripe tomatoes, chopped
Salt and black pepper to taste

Heat corn oil in large saucepan. Add zucchini, bell pepper, and onion. Stir and cook 5 minutes. Add garlic and okra; stir and cook 2 minutes. Add chopped tomatoes, salt and pepper. Add ½ cup water; bring to a boil. Reduce heat; simmer for about 20 minutes. Stir often. Add water if needed. Serve over hot cooked white rice. Serves 4.

CORNBREAD DRESSING

For Cornbread:
1 cup all-purpose flour
1 cup corn meal
½ teaspoon salt
1 teaspoon baking powder
1 egg
¼ cup corn oil
1 cup milk

½ cup chopped onion
½ cup chopped celery
½ cup chopped bell pepper
½ cup chopped green onion tops
1½ pounds chicken liver and
    giblets, finely-chopped
Salt and pepper to taste
1 cup cream of chicken soup

To make cornbread, mix together dry ingredients. Stir in egg, corn oil, and milk. Blend well. Pour into a greased 10-inch iron skillet. Bake in preheated 350-degree oven for 20 minutes or until golden brown. Saute' onion, celery, bell pepper, and green onion tops in additional margarine, using a medium saucepan; remove. Cook liver, giblets, and soup in same saucepan until meat is tender. Return onion mixture to saucepan. Add seasonings; mix well. Break the cornbread into pieces; place in baking dish. Top with soup mixture. Bake in 350-degree oven until texture is as dry as desired. Serves 8.

CRAWFISH DRESSING

1 pound cleaned crawfish tails
2 tablespoon corn oil
1 tablespoon butter
1 small onion, chopped
¼ bell pepper, chopped
2 cloves garlic, minced

1 cup cooked white rice
½ cup canned sliced mushrooms
1 tablespoon chopped parsley
¼ cup minced green onion tops
Salt, black and red pepper
Buttered bread crumbs

Coarsely chop crawfish tails. Heat oil and butter in large skillet. Add crawfish tails, chopped onion, bell pepper, and garlic. Stir and cook until wilted. Add rice, mushrooms, parsley, and green onion tops. Season to taste with salt, black and ground red pepper. Mix well. Use to stuff fish, or bake in a buttered casserole, topped with bread crumbs, at 375 degrees for 30 minutes. Serve as a side dish. Serves 4.

DIRTY RICE

¼ pound beef liver, chopped
½ cup chopped chicken giblets
¼ pound ground beef
¼ pound ground pork
Salt and black pepper to taste
3 tablespoons corn oil
1 medium onion, chopped

½ cup diced bell pepper
2 cloves garlic, chopped
¼ cup diced celery
½ cup water
4 cups cooked white rice
½ cup chopped parsley
½ cup chopped green onion tops

Cook liver and giblets in water until tender. Coat heavy skillet with additional corn oil. Season beef and pork with salt and pepper. Add to skillet; stir and cook until meat is done. Drain fat. Add 3 tablespoons corn oil to skillet. Add onion, bell pepper, garlic, and celery. Stir and cook until wilted. Add cooked meat. Stir in water; cover and simmer for 15 minutes. Add rice, parsley, and green onion tops. Mix well. Serve as a side dish, or use to stuff poultry. Serves 6 to 8.

This dish is humorously referred to as 'dirty rice' because of the appearance it takes when white rice, liver and giblets are combined. It's delicious!

OYSTER DRESSING

4 tablespoons corn oil
2 tablespoons flour
1 large onion, chopped
½ bell pepper, chopped
2 cloves garlic, minced
1 cup chopped celery

1 quart raw oysters, drained
4 cups cooked white rice
¼ cup minced parsley
½ cup minced green onion tops
Salt and black pepper to taste

Heat corn oil in heavy skillet. Gradually add flour, stirring constantly for 7 minutes—do not let roux burn. Add onion, bell pepper, garlic, and celery; stir and cook until tender. Add oysters. Cook until oysters curl and tests done. Remove skillet from heat. Add rice, parsley, green onion tops, and seasonings. Mix well. Serve hot as a side dish, or use to stuff poultry. Serves 6 to 8.

RICE STUFFING FOR FISH

3 tablespoons butter
¼ cup chopped onion
¼ cup chopped bell pepper
½ cup diced celery
2 tablespoons chopped parsley
½ pound cleaned raw shrimp

⅓ cup water or fish stock
1 cup raw oysters, chopped
1 teaspoon salt
⅛ teaspoon black pepper
Pinch ground red pepper
2 cups cooked white rice

Heat butter in heavy skillet. Add onion, bell pepper, and celery. Stir and cook until tender. Add parsley. Cut shrimp into small pieces; add to skillet. Stir and cook 2 minutes. Add water, oysters, salt and peppers. Bring to a boil. Reduce heat. Simmer for 20 minutes. Add rice; mix well. Serves 4.

BANANAS FOSTER

4 ripe bananas
10 tablespoons butter
½ cup brown sugar, packed
¼ teaspoon cinnamon

2 tablespoons banana liqueur,
   or 1 teaspoon vanilla extract
4 tablespoons rum
Vanilla ice cream

Peel bananas and cut in half lengthwise, then cut in half across. Heat butter in skillet over medium heat. Mix together sugar and cinnamon in a bowl. Add to butter; heat until sugar melts—stir occasionally. Add bananas and gently roll in mixture to coat well. Cook bananas 2 minutes, then gently turn them over; cook 1 minute. Pour liqueur over all. Heat rum in small saucepan, just enough to warm, then remove pan from heat; ignite. Pour over bananas. When flaming stops, serve sauce over a scoop of vanilla ice cream, with bananas on each side, in dessert dishes. Serves 4.

BEIGNETS

1 cup milk
2 tablespoons margarine
4 tablespoons sugar
½ teaspoon salt

1 egg, beaten
3 cups all-purpose flour
1 packet yeast

Heat milk over low heat. Add margarine, sugar, and salt; stir well; cool to lukewarm. Stir in egg. In large bowl, mix together 1½ cups flour and yeast. Add milk mixture; beat 5 minutes. Gradually add remaining flour. Form dough into a ball; place in greased bowl; turn to coat. Cover; chill in refrigerator for 4 hours. Pat out dough on floured pastry cloth. Cover and let stand 10 minutes. Roll out to form rectangles—3x2-inch is a good size. Cover and let stand 20 minutes. Deep-fry beignets in corn oil, a few at a time, until golden. Drain on paper towels. Sprinkle with powdered sugar. Makes 3 dozen.

There are different recipes for beignets. This one is meant to be served with coffee—others are served with syrup for breakfast, etc.

BLACKBERRY COBBLER

1 cup flour
3 teaspoons baking powder
1 cup sugar
⅛ teaspoon salt
1 cup evaporated milk
2 teaspoons vanilla

1 tablespoon cornstarch
¾ cup sugar
½ cup hot water
1 tablespoon fresh lemon juice
3 cups fresh blackberries
2 tablespoons butter

Mix together flour, baking powder, 1 cup sugar, and salt; blend well. Stir in milk and vanilla. Pour mixture into greased 7x11-inch glass baking dish. Mix together cornstarch and ¾ cup sugar. Add hot water; stir well. Add lemon juice and blackberries; mix well. Slowly pour into the center of batter. Dot with butter. Bake in 350-degree oven for 30 to 40 minutes. Serve warm with vanilla ice cream. Serves 8.

BUTTERMILK PIE

1 9-inch pie crust
1½ cups sugar
2 tablespoons flour
8 tablespoons butter, melted
1 cup buttermilk

3 large eggs, slightly beaten
2 teaspoons vanilla
1 tablespoon fresh lemon juice
⅛ teaspoon nutmeg
Pinch of salt, scant

Preheat oven to 475 degrees. Bake pie crust 5 minutes; cool. Mix together sugar and flour. Stir in butter. Add balance of ingredients; mix well. Pour mixture into pie shell. Bake in 350-degree oven for about 1 hour, or until knife inserted in center comes out clean. Makes 1 pie.

For an extra treat, serve topped with toasted slivered almonds, drizzled with hot fudge sauce!

COCONUT-LEMON DOBERGE CAKE

2½ cups all-purpose flour	1¾ cups sugar
3 teaspoons baking powder	3 eggs, separated
¼ teaspoon salt	2 teaspoons vanilla
½ cup butter	1 cup milk
4 tablespoons margarine	

Sift together flour, baking powder, and salt. Cream butter and margarine with sugar in large bowl; beat until fluffy. Beat in egg yolks and vanilla. Add dry ingredients alternately with milk; beat after each addition. Beat egg whites in small bowl until almost stiff; fold into batter. Pour equal amount of batter (about ¾ cup each pan) into 3 greased and floured 8-inch round cake pans. Do this twice, giving you 6 thin layers. (Wash and prepare pans for second baking the same as for first baking.) Bake in preheated 375-degree oven about 10 to 12 minutes, or until a toothpick inserted in center comes out clean. Cool in pan a little; remove and cool on rack. Spread following filling between layers. Then spread following icing over cake.

*See next page for filling and icing recipes.

DOBERGE CAKE FILLING

1½ cups sugar
3 tablespoons cornstarch
2 tablespoons flour
⅛ teaspoon salt
1¼ cups water

3 egg yolks, beaten
2 tablespoons butter
½ cup lemon juice
2 teaspoons vanilla
¾ cup coconut

Mix together sugar, cornstarch, flour, and salt in saucepan. Stir in water. Cook, stirring constantly until thickened. Quickly stir in egg yolks. Add butter; cook and stir about 3 minutes. Stir in lemon juice, vanilla, and coconut.

ICING:

Stir together ⅓ cup melted butter, 2 cups powdered sugar, 1½ teaspoon vanilla, and about 3 tablespoons hot water; add more water if too thick; add more sugar if too thin.

You can make this cake baking 3 regular layers. Cool and split the layers in half, giving your 6 layers, and no extra pans to wash!

LES OREILLES DE COCHON

2 cups all-purpose flour
1½ teaspoons baking powder
½ teaspoon salt
2 eggs
8 tablespoons butter, melted and cooled

½ teaspoon vanilla
Corn oil for deep frying
1 cup pure cane syrup
1 cup fresh-picked Louisiana pecans, chopped

Mix together flour, baking powder, and salt. In a large bowl, beat eggs until frothy. Beat in butter. Stir in vanilla. Beat in half of the dry ingredients, then stir in balance by hand. Form into a large ball, then divide into 24 small balls. Roll out on floured surface to form paper-thin circle. Heat oil in deep, heavy pot to 375 degrees; drop in one or two pieces of rolled dough at a time. As soon as dough rises to top, give a swift twist to center of dough with a long-handle fork, this forms the shape of the ear. Fry until brown. Drain on paper towels. Bring syrup to a boil in a small saucepan; cook until a soft ball forms when dropped in water. Place pastries on buttered platter; drizzle with hot syrup. Sprinkle with pecans. Makes 24.

Les oreilles de cochon means pig ear in French—the pastry is so named because it resembles the shape of the ear.

PECAN BRITTLE

2 cups sugar
3 cups broken pecans
¾ cups white corn syrup

¼ cup water
3 teaspoons baking soda

Combine all ingredients, except baking soda, in a large heavy saucepan. Cook over medium heat, stirring constantly until candy thermometer registers 290 degrees. Stir in baking soda quickly—mixture will foam up! Pour onto greased cookie sheet and spread with greased spatula. Allow to cool throughly, about two hours; break into pieces. Store in an air-tight container. Makes a little over 1 pound.

PECAN PIE

5 tablespoons butter
¾ cup sugar
3 eggs, slightly beaten
¾ cup dark Karo corn syrup
¼ teaspoon salt

1½ teaspoons vanilla
¾ cup coarsely chopped pecans
½ cup flaked coconut
Pecan halves for top
1 9-inch unbaked pie crust

Cream butter and sugar; beat until light and fluffy. Add eggs, syrup, salt, vanilla, chopped pecans, and coconut. Mix well. Pour into pie crust. Top with pecan halves. Bake in preheated 400-degree oven for 10 minutes. Reduce heat to 350 degrees; bake about 40 minutes. Serve with vanilla ice cream. Makes 1 pie.

PECAN YAM MUFFINS

1¾ cups all-purpose flour
3 teaspoons baking powder
½ teaspoon salt
1 teaspoon cinnamon
½ teaspoon nutmeg
½ cup sugar
2 tablespoons brown sugar
1 egg

1 cup milk
1 cup freshly-baked yams,
cooled and mashed
¼ cup butter or margarine
¾ cup chopped pecans
2 teaspoons grated fresh orange
rind
Extra sugar and cinnamon

Mix together dry ingredients in large bowl. Blend well. Beat egg in another bowl; stir in milk, yams, and butter. Add pecans and orange rind to flour mixture. Add flour mixture to egg mixture. Stir only until moistened—batter should be lumpy. Spoon into greased muffin pan, filling each cup about ½ full. Mix together extra 1 teaspoon sugar and ⅛ teaspoon cinnamon and sprinkle a little over each muffin. Bake in preheated 400-degree oven 20 to 25 minutes. Remove from pan. Serve warm with butter. Makes 1 dozen.

PRALINES

1 cup brown sugar	2 tablespoons dark corn syrup
1 cup sugar	2 tablespoons butter
1/8 teaspoon salt	1 teaspoon vanilla
1/2 cup evaporated milk	2 1/4 cups pecan halves

In a large saucepan, mix together sugars, salt, milk, and syrup. Stir and cook over medium heat until soft-ball stage is reached. Remove pan from heat. Add butter, vanilla, and pecans. Beat until just beginning to thicken, about 3 minutes. Drop by heaping tablespoonfuls onto waxed paper, forming a flat, round praline. Let harden. Makes about 18.

PRALINE COOKIES

¾ cup butter, do not substitute
1½ cups brown sugar, packed
1 egg

1 teaspoon vanilla
1½ cups sifted all-purpose flour
1 cup chopped pecans

Cream butter until smooth. Add sugar and egg. Beat until smooth and fluffy. Add vanilla. Sift in flour; blend throughly. Stir in pecans. Shape into balls, using 1 level tablespoon of dough for each. On a buttered baking sheet, flatten balls to ⅛-inch thickness, spacing 1-inch apart. Bake in preheated 375-degree oven for 10 to 12 minutes, or until nicely browned. Cool in pan a minute. Transfer to cooling rack. Makes 3 dozen.

SPICED FRUIT BREAD PUDDING

2 cups dry bread cubes
4 cups milk, scalded
¾ cup sugar
1 tablespoon butter
¼ teaspoon salt
¼ teaspoon nutmeg

⅛ teaspoon cinnamon
⅛ teaspoon ginger
4 eggs, lightly beaten
2 teaspoons vanilla
¼ cup light raisins
½ cup drained pineapple

Soak bread in milk 5 minutes. Pour over balance of ingredients; mix well. Pour mixture into a buttered 1½-quart glass baking dish. Place in a pan of hot water. Bake in 350-degree oven for 1 hour, or until knife inserted in center comes out clean. Serve with following custard sauce. Serves 8.

See page 99 for custard sauce.

CUSTARD SAUCE

1½ cups milk
4 egg yolks
¼ cup sugar

¼ teaspoon salt
⅛ teaspoon nutmeg
1½ teaspoons vanilla

Scald milk in top of double boiler. In a small bowl beat together egg yolks, sugar, salt, and nutmeg. Gradually add to milk, stirring constantly until sauce thickens and forms a thin coating on a metal spoon. Remove from heat. Cool quickly. Stir in vanilla. Chill throughly. Serve on top of warm spiced bread pudding.

SWEET POTATO PIE

2 cups cooked and mashed
   sweet potatoes
¾ cup sugar
½ cup coconut
1 cup chopped pecans
2 tablespoons melted butter
2 teaspoons vanilla

½ cup heavy cream
⅓ teaspoon salt
3 eggs, beaten
½ teaspoon cinnamon
1 tablespoon brandy, optional
1 unbaked pie crust

In a large bowl, stir together all ingredients, except pie crust, until well-blended. Pour into unbaked pie crust. Bake in preheated 450-degree oven for 10 minutes. Reduce heat to 350 degrees. Bake about 35 minutes, or until knife inserted in center comes out clean. Cool; cover with meringue: Beat 3 egg whites until frothy. Gradually add ⅓ cup sugar. Beat until stiff. Beat in ½ teaspoon lemon extract. Pile on pie. Brown in 325-degree oven about 15 minutes. Chill before serving. Refrigerate. Makes 1 pie.

TURTLES

¼ cup butter
1 cup evaporated milk
1 cup sugar
1 cup dark corn syrup
¼ teaspoon salt

1 teaspoon vanilla
120 pecan halves
1 6-oz. package sem-sweet
  chocolate chips
1 teaspoon solid shortening

Heat butter and milk in a small saucepan until butter is melted. In a separate 2-quart saucepan, cook sugar, corn syrup, and salt over medium heat , stirring often, until it reaches firm-ball stage (244 degrees F. on candy thermometer). Remove from heat. Stir in vanilla. Cool to room temperature. On waxed paper, arrange 5 pecan halves per turtle: 1 for the head, 3 for the body, and 1 for the tail. Put about 1 teaspoon caramel on each pecan. Let stand until firm. Melt chocolate chips, using a double boiler. Add 1 teaspoon solid shortening; stir until blended. Spread on top to cover caramel on each turtle. Cool until firm. Makes 2 dozen.

WINTER PEACH COBBLER

¼ cup butter
1 cup all-purpose flour
1 cup sugar
⅛ teaspoon salt
1 tablespoon baking powder
⅔ cup milk

1 16-oz. can sliced peaches
1½ teaspoons vanilla
¼ teaspoon nutmeg
½ teaspoon cinnamon, scant
1 fresh lemon, cut in half

Melt butter in 7x11-inch shallow glass baking dish in oven. In a bowl, sift together flour, sugar, salt, and baking powder. Add milk and stir well. Pour into baking dish—*do not stir*. Top with peaches, including juice—*do not stir*. Drizzle evenly with vanilla. Sprinkle evenly with nutmeg and cinnamon. Lemon in hand, squeeze fresh lemon juice over all, using about ¾ of the whole lemon—*do not stir*. Bake in preheated 350-degree oven 40 minutes, or until golden brown on top. Serve warm with vanilla ice cream. Serves 6.

ROUX

½ cup corn oil   ½ cup all-purpose flour

Heat oil in a small heavy skillet. Add flour, stirring constantly over medium heat until brown, about 15 minutes. Reduce heat and continue stirring and cooking if a darker roux is desired. Take roux out of the skillet—or roux will continue to cook.

The roux is very important in Cajun-Creole cooking. If you burn the roux, discard it and start a fresh one—the dish will have a bitter flavor if you use a roux that has been burned.

CAFE AU LAIT

3 tablespoons sugar
3 cups light cream or milk

2 cups hot fresh coffee

Heat sugar in heavy saucepan until caramelized. Remove from heat and place in a sugar bowl. Heat cream or milk over low heat; beat with an egg beater until it foams. Pour into a serving pot. Put sugar in serving cups; pour equal amounts of hot coffee and hot cream or milk over sugar. Serves 4.

CREOLE COFFEE

4 cups water, boiling hot   **8 tablespoons coffee**

Select a dark roast, medium-ground coffee. Use a small drip coffee pot. When water is boiling, use a dipper to pour a small amount of water on coffee grounds; allow grounds to stop bubbling and settle each time before pouring on a dipper full of boiling water again. When coffee is made, place pot in a small pan of hot water. Heat piping hot, but do not boil coffee. For best flavor, make coffee fresh each time you serve it—do not serve old coffee. Serve in demitassee (half cup) with cream and sugar. Serves 8.

HUSH PUPPIES

1½ cups yellow cornmeal	⅛ teaspoon black pepper
½ cup all-purpose flour	2 eggs, beaten
2 tablespoons sugar	½ cup minced onion
3 teaspoons baking powder	1 cup milk
¼ teaspoon salt	Corn oil

Combine dry ingredients; mix well. Add eggs, onion, and milk. Stir to make a stiff batter. Heat corn oil in deep, heavy pot. Drop batter by tablespoonfuls into hot oil—not less than 4-inches deep. Fry until golden brown, about 2 minutes. Drain on paper towels. Makes about 3 dozen.

Add finely-chopped cooked shrimp to batter for variation.

FRENCH BREAD

1 packet dry yeast	1½ teaspoons salt
1¼ cups warm water	1 egg white beaten with
2 teaspoons sugar	1 teaspoon water
3 cups all-purpose flour	Corn meal

Dissolve yeast with sugar in warm water (115 degrees) in mixing bowl. Stir in 2 cups flour and salt. Beat 3 minutes with electric mixer until smooth. Stir in enough flour by hand to handle dough easily. Knead on a lightly-floured surface until smooth and elastic, about 10 minutes; add flour if needed. Shape into a ball; place into greased bowl; turn to coat. Cover; let rise in warm place until double, about 2 hours. Punch down; cover and let rest 10 minutes. Divide dough in half. Roll into two 8x16-inch rectangles. Roll up tightly starting at 16-inch side. Pinch dough to seal seam; taper ends. Place seam-side down on greased cookie sheet sprinkled with corn meal. Make 3 slashes with sharp knife about ¼ inch deep on top. Brush with cold water. Let rise until double. Brush with egg white. Bake in preheated 375-degree oven about 40 to 45 minutes. Brush with egg white once in middle of baking period. Makes 2 small loaves.

eresa N. Millang, author of *The Best of Cajun-Creole Recipes*, is a native of Louisiana, home of Cajun-Creole cooking—a cuisine that is sweeping the country. Here are recipes for classics such as gumbo, jambalaya, crawfish, red beans, and okra, as well as new like blackened redfish! Theresa published her first Cajun cookbook, *Roux Roux Roux*, in 1986. She is the author of three other cookbooks, *The Muffins Are Coming, The Cookies Are Coming,* and *The Brownies are Coming*. Theresa now lives in Minnesota.

**Adventure
Publications**
1-800-678-7006

ISBN
0-934860-93-9

ISBN 0-934860-93-9

50595>

9 780934 860932